SPACE EXPLORERS

OUR UNIVERSE

Giles Sparrow

Published in 2018 by Enslow Publishing, LLC.
101 W. 23rd Street, Suite 240, New York, NY 10011

Library of Congress Cataloging-in-Publication Data

Names: Sparrow, Giles, 1970- author.
Title: Our universe / Giles Sparrow.
Description: New York : Enslow Publishing, 2018. | Series: Space explorers | Audience: K to grade 3. | Includes bibliographical references and index.
Identifiers: LCCN 2017016824| ISBN 9780766092631 (library bound) | ISBN 9780766093287 (pbk.) | ISBN 9780766094031 (6 pack)
Subjects: LCSH: Cosmology—Juvenile literature. | Galaxies—Juvenile literature. | Universe—Juvenile literature.
Classification: LCC QB983 S665 2018 | DDC 523.1—dc23
LC record available at https://lccn.loc.gov/2017016824

Printed in the United States of America

To Our Readers: We have done our best to make sure all websites in this book were active and appropriate when we went to press. However, the author and the publisher have no control over and assume no liability for the material available on those websites or on any websites they may link to. Any comments or suggestions can be sent by e-mail to customerservice@enslow.com.

Picture Credits:
Key: b-bottom, t-top, c-center, l-left, r-right Alamy: 12-13 (NG Images); ESA: 22br (C Carreau); ESO: 20br (Hubble Space Telescope); Getty Images: 10br (Jon Brenneis); TH Jarrett: 7b (IPAC/SSC); NASA: 6br, 11tr & 26cr (WMAP Science Team), 14c & 26br & 31bc (JPL-Caltech/Las Campanas Observatory), 17tr (CXC/Stanford/I Zhuravleva et al.), 18c & 27tl & 30-31b (Spitzer Space Telescope), 20-21 (Chandra X-ray Observatory Center), 21cr (Fermi), 23c & 27bl (NASA/CXC/CfA/M Markevitch et al./STScl/ Magellan/ASU/D Clowe et al., ESO WFI), 24br (JPL/ASU); Shutterstock: cover & title page main (MaraQu), tl (NikoNomad), c (chaoss), bl (GiroScience), tr (Jurik Peter), br (Triff), 4-5 (Stefano Garau), 4cl (MaraQu), 4b (Viktar Malyshchyts), 4cr (NASA), 5t (tose), 5br (pixbox77), 6-7 & 26tr (MaraQu), 8-9 & 26tl & 31tr (chaoss), 8bl (Matt Ragen), 10-11 (Designua), 12br & 26bl (vectortatu), 14-15 (NASA), 16-17 (Denis Belitsky), 16c &26tr (chainfoto24), 18-19 (NASA), 19tl (Giovanni Benintende), 20cl & 27cr & 30t (Igor Zh), 24-25 (breakermaximus), 24c & 27br (Mopic), 25ct (Phongsak Meedaenphai), 28 (Denis Belitsky), 29t (Bill Frische), 29b (solarseven); Springel et al.: 22-23; Wikimedia Commons: 8tr.

Enslow Publishing
101 W. 23rd Street
Suite 240
New York, NY 10011
USA
enslow.com

CONTENTS

Introduction

Our Universe is a huge area of space made up of everything we can see in every direction. It contains a great number of different objects—from tiny specks of cosmic dust to mighty galaxy superclusters. The most interesting of these are planets, stars and nebulae, galaxies, and clusters of galaxies.

Stars

A star is a dense (tightly packed) ball of gas that shines through chemical reactions in its core (middle). Our Sun is a star. Stars range from red dwarfs, much smaller and fainter than the Sun, to supergiants a hundred times larger and a million times brighter.

Planets

A planet is a large ball of rock or gas that orbits (travels around) a star. In our solar system there are eight "major" planets, several dwarf planets, and countless smaller objects. These range from asteroids and comets down to tiny specks of dust.

Nebulae

The space between the stars is filled with mostly unseen clouds of gas and dust called nebulae. Where they collapse (fall in) and grow dense enough to form new stars, they light up from within.

Galaxies

A galaxy is a huge cloud of stars, gas, and dust, including nebulae, held together by a force called gravity. There are many different types of galaxy. This is because their shape, the nature of their stars, and the amount of gas and dust within them can vary.

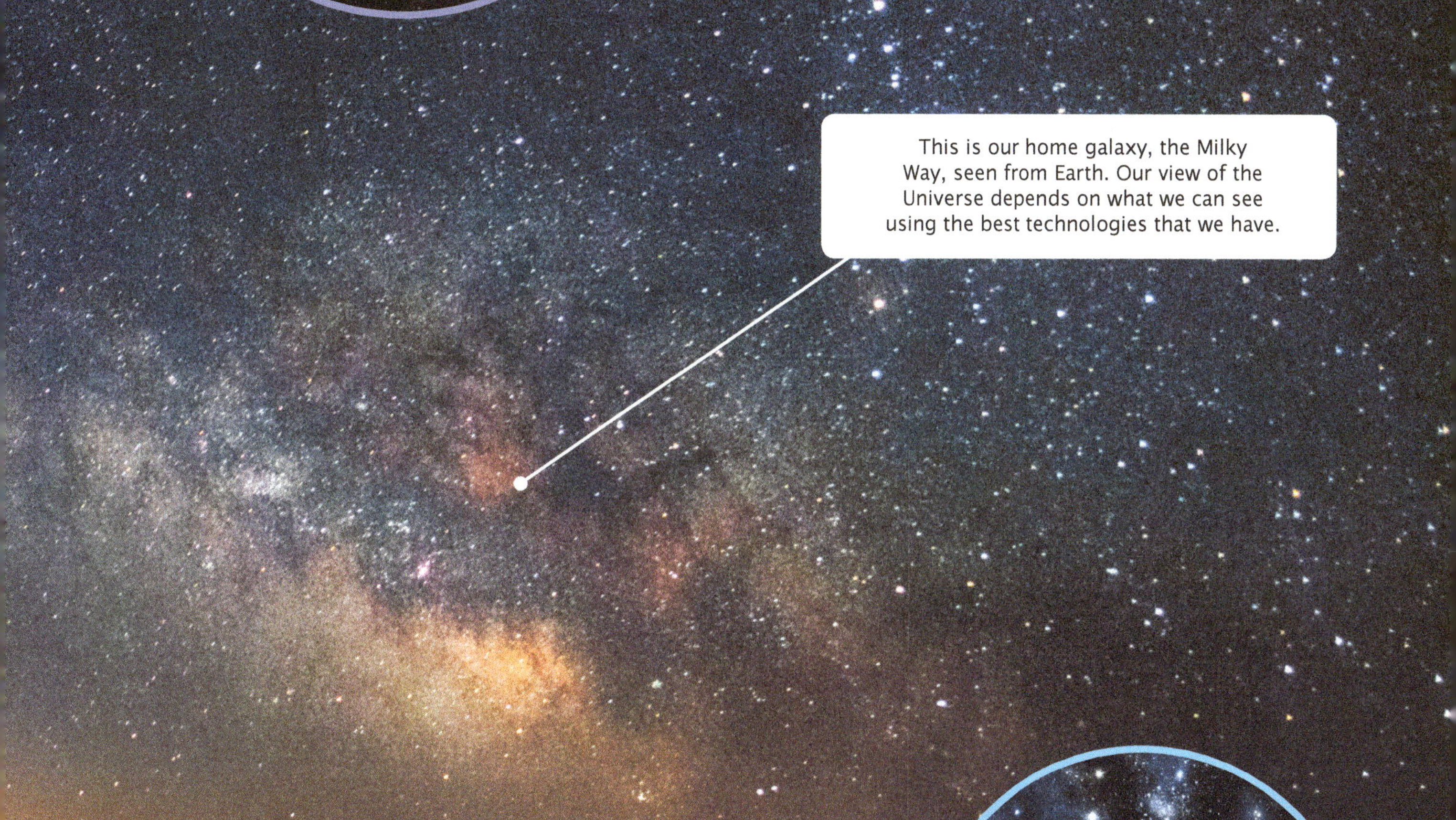

This is our home galaxy, the Milky Way, seen from Earth. Our view of the Universe depends on what we can see using the best technologies that we have.

Galaxy Clusters

Gravity makes galaxies bunch together to form clusters that are millions of light-years wide. These clusters join together at the edges to form even bigger superclusters—the largest structures in the Universe.

The Universe

Our Universe is a massive area of space that stretches farther than we can see in every direction. It has more galaxies, stars, and planets than we could ever hope to count, and huge amounts of other material, most of which is invisible to even our most powerful telescopes.

Looking Back in Time

We can only see objects in other parts of the Universe thanks to the light and other radiation we see in our telescopes. Light is the fastest thing in the Universe, so we measure huge distances in space in light-years (the distance light travels in a year, which is 5.9 trillion miles or 9.5 trillion km). The farther away object is in the Universe, the longer its light has taken to reach Earth, and the farther back in time we are seeing.

We see far-away parts of space as they were thousands or even millions of years ago, when their light set out toward us.

Curved Space

It might be hard to imagine, but space can be curved in different directions by objects with mass (weight and density). This is the basis of the force of gravity. An easier way to think about this is to imagine space as a flat rubber sheet—heavy objects create a dent within the sheet, and this will change the paths of any other objects passing nearby.

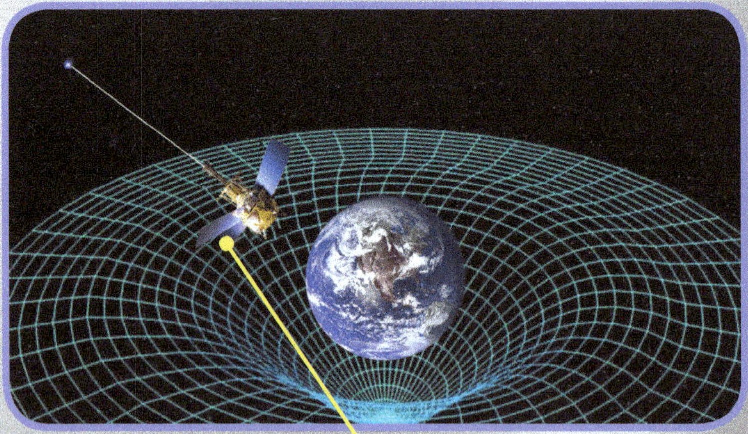

A satellite's orbit around a planet such as Earth stops it from "falling" into the curved space created by Earth's mass.

Stars, gas, and dust are the main visible parts of our Universe. Other objects are hard to detect (make out).

Five-sixths of matter in the Universe is dark matter, which we cannot see or measure.

This map shows where the 45,000 galaxies in our small part of the Universe are.

Big Bang

Our Universe was born 13.8 billion years ago in a huge explosion called the Big Bang. The event not only created all the matter in the Universe, but also spacc and timc, so it is meaningless to ask where it happened, or what happened before.

Discovery

The Russian scientist Alexander Friedmann was the first person to suggest that the Universe might be expanding (growing), in 1924. The American Edwin Hubble proved this in 1929. The Belgian Georges Lemaître followed the expansion backward and stated that the Universe began in a hot, dense ball of matter.

Alexander Friedmann, the first scientist to work on the idea of an expanding Universe.

The Large Hadron Collider is a machine that recreates what the Universe was like during the Big Bang, in a much smaller space.

The Beginning

The Big Bang released huge amounts of pure energy, but as the Universe expanded, it cooled quickly and the energy was locked up within the tiniest of particles. Over the first few minutes, these particles joined together until they formed the building blocks of atoms. Atoms are the smallest particles that make up chemical elements.

13.8 BILLION YEARS AGO	+1 SECOND	+20 MINUTES	+380,000 YEARS	+150 MILLION YEARS
The Big Bang creates all matter and energy in the Universe.	Energy changes into the tiniest of particles.	Heavy particles group together to form the cores of atoms. Small particles called electrons stay on the loose. Light waves are trapped in the fog of particles.	Electrons combine with nuclei to form first atoms. Fog clears and the Universe becomes transparent.	First stars and quasar galaxies begin to form.

Galaxies and stars formed about 150 million years after the Big Bang itself.
The Universe is a huge expanding bubble, but there is no way of getting outside it.
During the Big Bang, energy could change into mass and back, creating the building blocks of matter.

Expanding Universe

The farther away we look in space, the faster things are rushing away from us in all directions. It is a sign that the Universe as a whole is expanding, just as we would expect if it started as the explosion of the Big Bang.

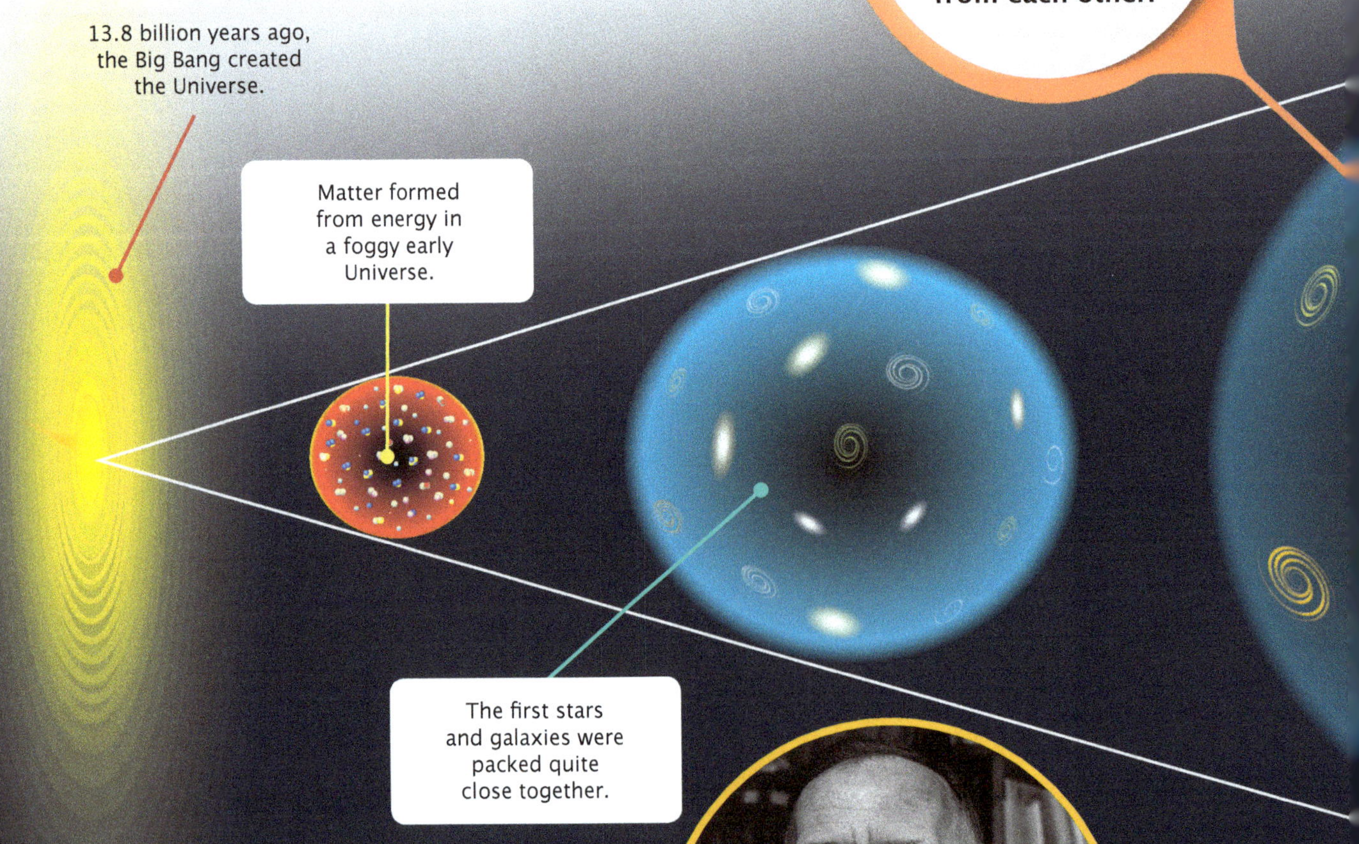

Hubble's Law

In the mid-1920s, Edwin Hubble used a very clever way to find the distance to other galaxies. In 1929, he compared these distances to measurements of the way the galaxies moved, and found an amazing pattern—the farther away a galaxy is, the faster it is moving away from us.

Edwin Hubble discovered the expanding Universe.

Cosmic Background

Short radio waves called microwaves, coming from every part of the Universe, are called cosmic background radiation. Discovered in 1964, they are left over from the Big Bang itself, and hold important information about the growing Universe.

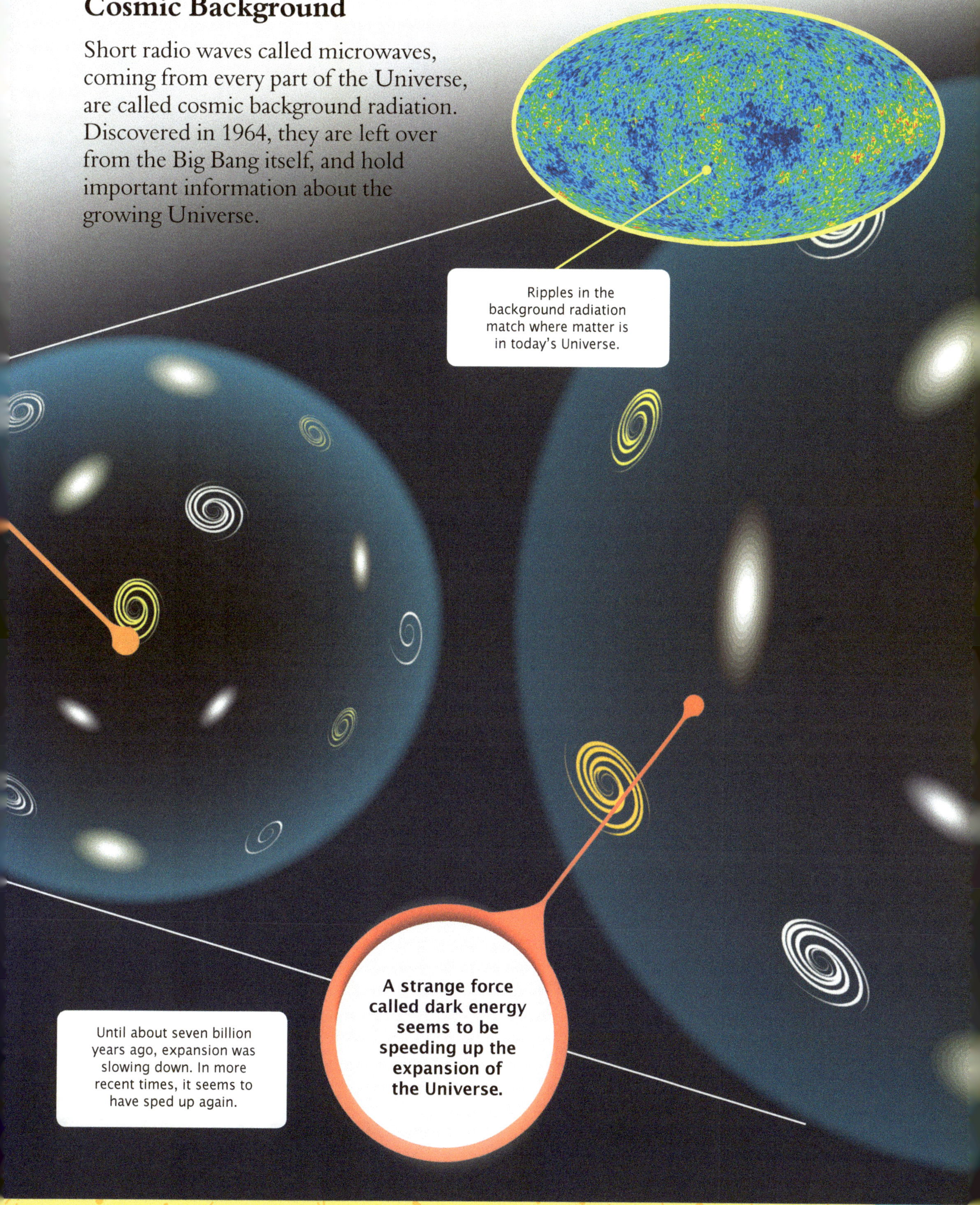

Galaxies

Galaxies are groups of stars, gas, and dust. Some are huge balls of trillions of stars and others are small clouds of just a few million. Pulled together by the force of gravity, these clouds become factories for making new stars.

Crowded Universe

Galaxies are huge objects—tens or even hundreds of thousands of light-years across, and with powerful gravity that have an effect on the galaxies nearest to them. This means that they tend to crowd together in some places, forming clusters of anything from tens to thousands of galaxies. On the largest scales, clusters join together to form superclusters that are hundreds of millions of light-years wide.

This "Hubble Deep Field" holds 5,500 galaxies.

Galaxy Types

Astronomers group galaxies into many different kinds. The most important are spirals (disks with spiral arms where the brightest stars are close together) and ellipticals (balls of red and yellow stars that look like the middle of spirals). There are also irregulars (shapeless clouds, often made up of many bright stars).

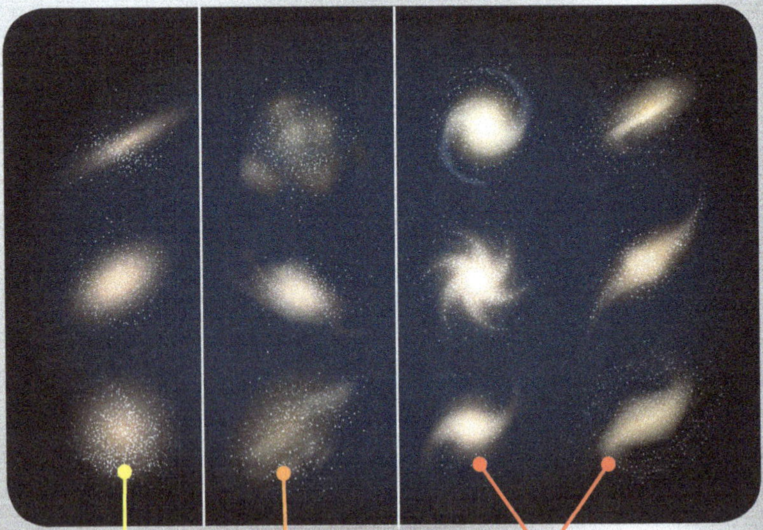

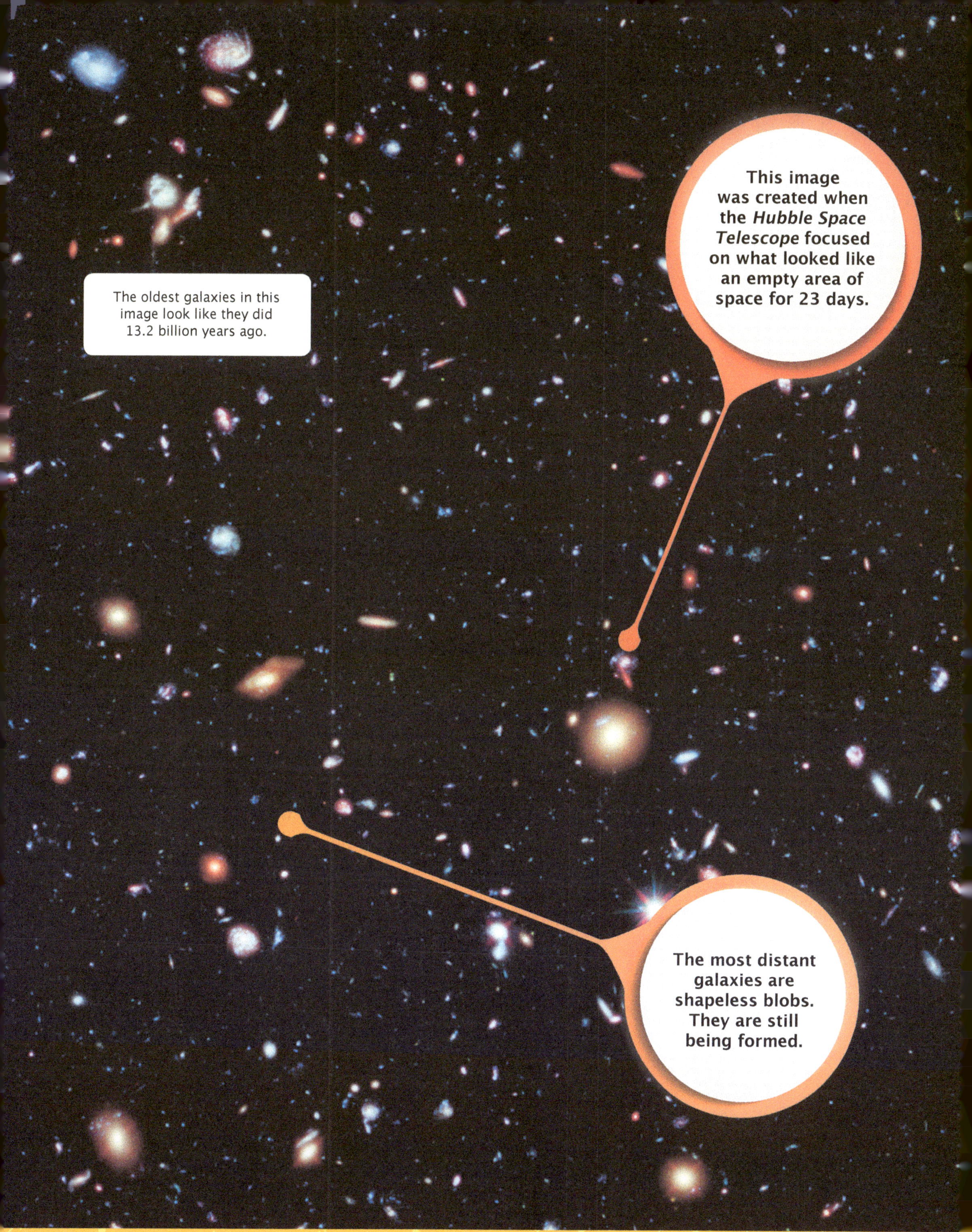
The oldest galaxies in this image look like they did 13.2 billion years ago.
This image was created when the *Hubble Space Telescope* focused on what looked like an empty area of space for 23 days.
The most distant galaxies are shapeless blobs. They are still being formed.

How Galaxies Form

All the different types of galaxy are related to each other by how they developed. Over billions of years, galaxies join together and change type, then slowly change back—or change into something else entirely.

Galactic Chaos

Compared with objects such as stars or planets, galaxies are quite closely packed together. Collisions (crashes) happen often. When galaxies hit each other, gravity can change the orbits of stars, creating a chaotic cloud of stars that takes a long time to settle back down.

New Stars, Old Stars

Galaxies can only form new stars if they have enough of the raw materials—gas and dust clouds. When galaxies crash again and again, the gas heats up until it is too fast-moving to form new stars. This is why old ball-shaped elliptical (oval) galaxies have very little gas and no new or young stars—they mostly have long-lived, red and yellow stars.

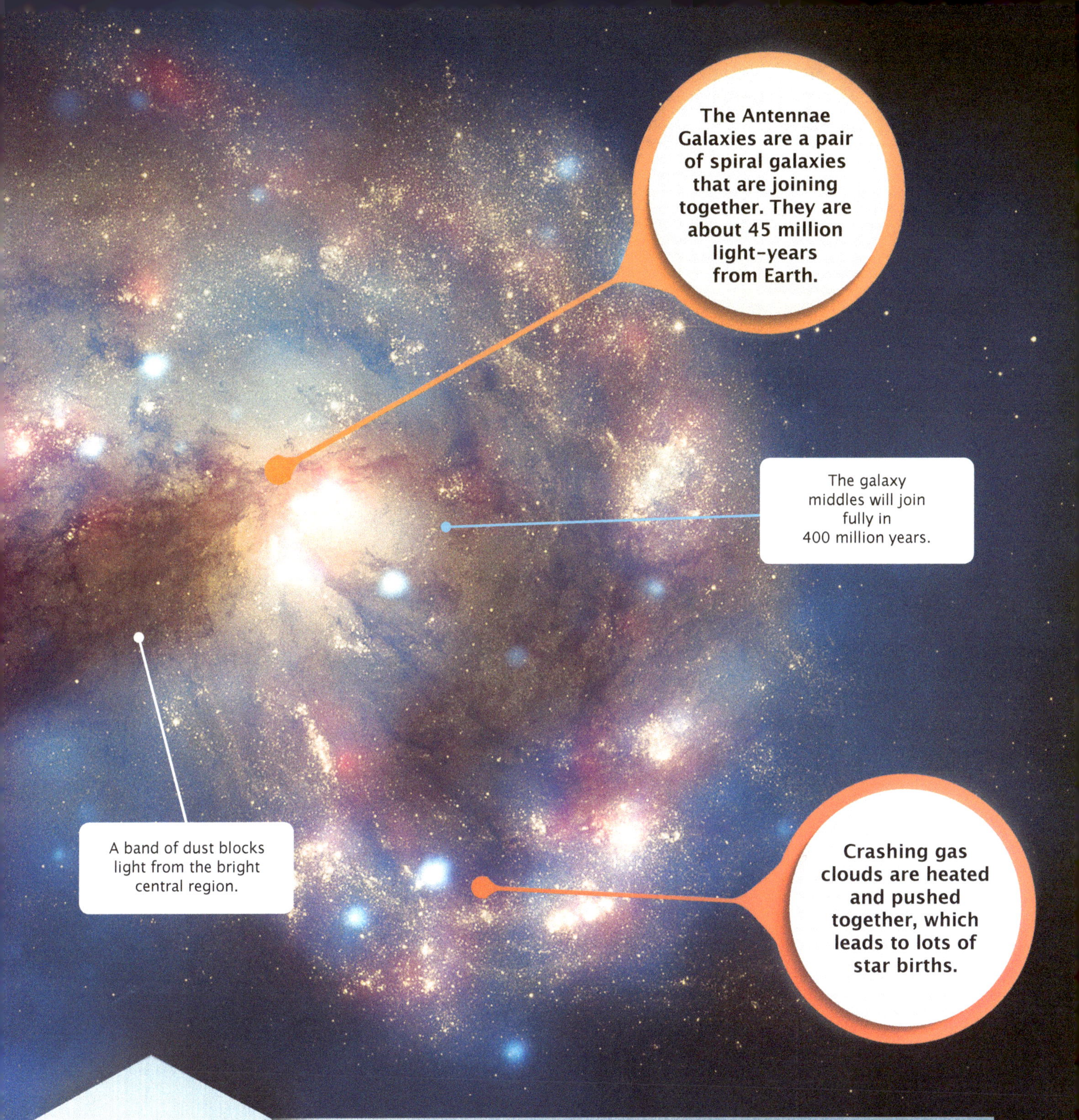

GALAXY PROFILE

Name: Antennae Galaxies
Catalogue numbers: NGC 4038 & NGC 4039
Constellation: Corvus
Distance from Earth: 55 million light-years
Description: A pair of colliding spiral galaxies with unwound spiral arms in the shape of an insect's antennae

Milky Way

Binoculars or a telescope show that the Milky Way is made up of countless faint stars that seem close together in the sky.

Our home galaxy, the Milky Way, is a large spiral with a bar of stars across its middle. Our solar system orbits in the flattened disk, in the middle of two of the spiral arms and about 27,000 light-years from the star clouds that form the heart of the galaxy.

Band Across the Sky

From Earth, we see the Milky Way as a band of light that wraps around the night sky. Because of its disk shape, we see more stars when we look across the disk, and many fewer when we look "up" or "down" out of the disk. The band is brightest where we look toward the middle of the galaxy.

The middle of the Milky Way lies in the constellation Sagittarius, hidden behind dense clouds of stars and dust.

Dark Secret

The orbits of stars close to the middle of the Milky Way show something surprising—they are moving very fast around a huge object with the mass of millions of Suns. Astronomers think that this object, which can't be seen directly through any telescope, is a huge black hole formed early in the Milky Way's history. Everything orbits around it.

GALAXY PROFILE

Name: Milky Way
Diameter: 120,000 light-years
Mass: Approx 1,200 billion Suns
Number of stars: Approx 200 billion
Distance to centre: 27,000 light-years
Description: Spiral galaxy with four spiral arms and a central bar of stars

This image shows a flash of X-rays from the area around the Milky Way's central black hole. It could mark the last moments of an asteroid that moved too close and was pulled in.

The Milky Way is about 120,000 light-years across, but just 2,000 light-years thick.

Dark patches in the Milky Way are created by dust clouds that are blocking out more distant stars.

Nearby Galaxies

The Milky Way is one of about 50 galaxies in a small, loose cluster (group) that astronomers call the Local Group. The cluster is about ten million light-years across, and is mostly made up of three large galaxies—the Milky Way, and the Andromeda and Triangulum spirals.

The Tarantula Nebula is a huge cloud of star-forming gas and dust in the Large Magellanic Cloud.

Ruled by Gravity

The Local Group is an area of space where the gravity of these three galaxies is slowly pulling everything together. For example, the Milky Way and Andromeda galaxies are being drawn toward an unavoidable crash that will mean they join together in about five billion years.

This infrared image shows the Large Magellanic Cloud as a place where a lot of stars are born.

Satellite Galaxies

The brightest galaxies of the Local Group are two irregular galaxies called the Large and Small Magellanic Clouds.

Visible from Earth's southern hemisphere, they look like separate clumps of the Milky Way, but are actually in orbit around it at distances of 160,000 and 200,000 light-years. The shapes of both are changed by our galaxy's huge gravity.

GALAXY PROFILE

Name: Large Magellanic Cloud (LMC)
Constellation: Dorado and Mensa
Distance from Earth: 160,000 light-years
Size: 15,000 light-years wide
Description: A galaxy with some signs of a spiral structure, including a central bar

Andromeda is our closest large galaxy. It is a spiral galaxy, about the same size as the Milky Way.
Wind from newborn stars has blown away gas from around them.
Central cluster of newborn monster stars.

Strange Galaxies

Quite a lot of galaxies seem to release more radiation—both light and other types—than their stars alone are able to. Astronomers call these "active galaxies," and they think their activity comes from a monster black hole tearing matter apart.

The core of galaxy M106 appears bright because of its active nucleus.

Different Kinds of Activity

When astronomers first found active galaxies, they thought they were looking at many different objects. Some galaxies have huge clouds of radio waves around them; others seem quite normal except for a slightly brighter core. The most impressive are quasars, where the core shines so brightly that the light of the galaxy around it can't be seen.

A quasar has a brightly shining disk at its core.

Centaurus A is a nearby "radio galaxy."

Heart of the Matter

The different types of galaxy are all formed because of an object called an active galactic nucleus. This is a central area where stars, gas, and dust are being pulled into a giant black hole. As they are, they form a superhot disk that releases very bright light and other radiations. Jets of particles "spat out" from above and below the disk billow out into huge clouds of radio waves.

GALAXY PROFILE

Name: Messier 106
Constellation: Canes Venatici
Distance from Earth: 23.5 million light-years
Diameter: 60,000 light-years
Description: A distorted spiral "Seyfert" galaxy with an unusually bright core

Dark Matter

One of the strangest things about our Universe is that everything we see and measure is just a tiny part of everything there is. The visible Universe of stars and galaxies is dwarfed by five times as much dark matter, a strange substance that doesn't release or take in radiation of any kind. This makes it totally invisible.

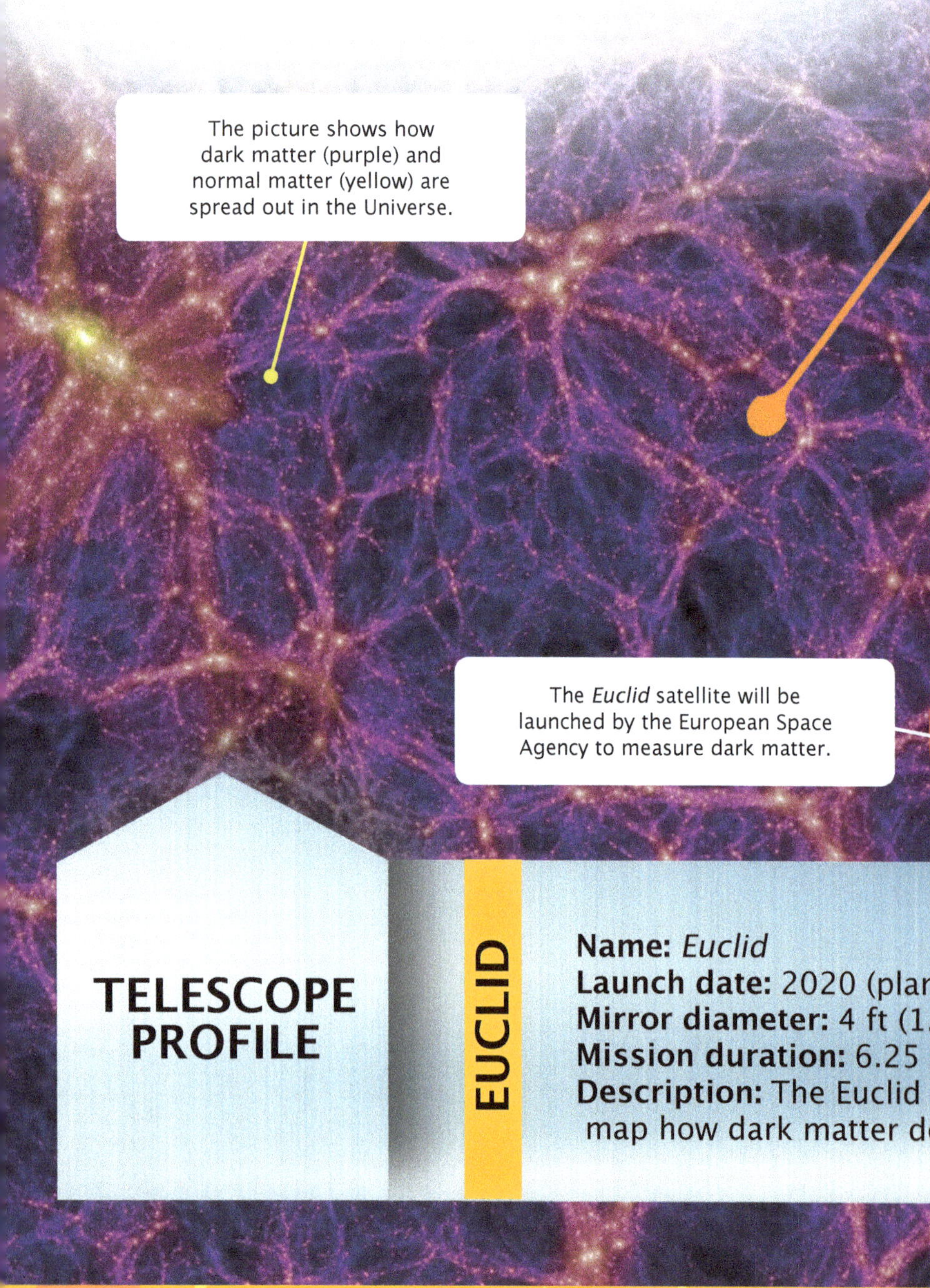

Pictures like this one, created on a computer, help scientists to work out where dark matter is compared to visible objects, such as galaxy clusters.

The picture shows how dark matter (purple) and normal matter (yellow) are spread out in the Universe.

The *Euclid* satellite will be launched by the European Space Agency to measure dark matter.

TELESCOPE PROFILE

EUCLID

Name: *Euclid*
Launch date: 2020 (planned)
Mirror diameter: 4 ft (1.2 m)
Mission duration: 6.25 years
Description: The Euclid mission will map how dark matter deflects light

What is Dark Matter?

Astronomers used to think there were two possible explanations for dark matter. Small, dense clumps of "normal matter" such as planets and black holes might be too dark for our telescopes to discover, or there could be a completely different type of particle unknown to science. In the past few years it has become clear that unseen normal matter cannot add up to the amount of matter that must make up the Universe, so the hunt is on for strange new particles.

Telltale Traces

Dark matter can be found through gravity. It was first discovered by the way it changed the movement of stars and galaxies. Today astronomers can also find out where it is by looking at the way that it bends space and deflects (changes the path of) light from far-away galaxies.

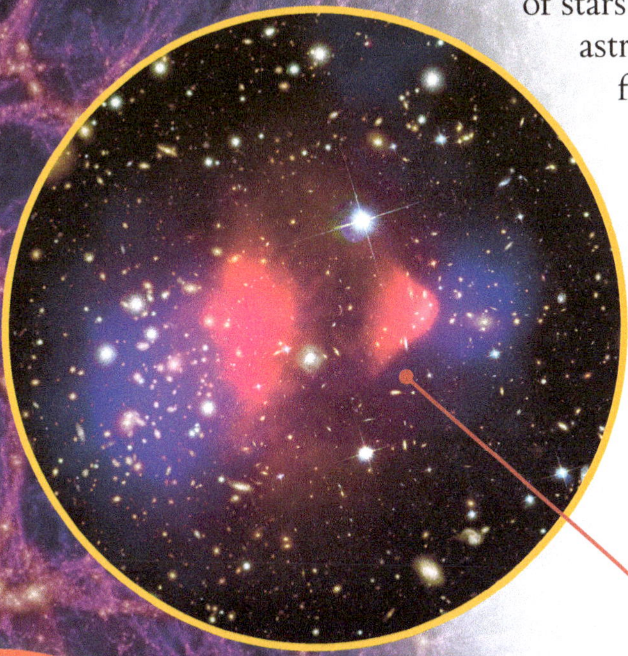

This map shows where galaxies (yellow), hot gas (pink), and dark matter (blue) are in a galaxy cluster called the Bullet.

Gravity from large areas of dark matter in the early Universe may have decided where galaxy clusters and superclusters developed.

Alien Life

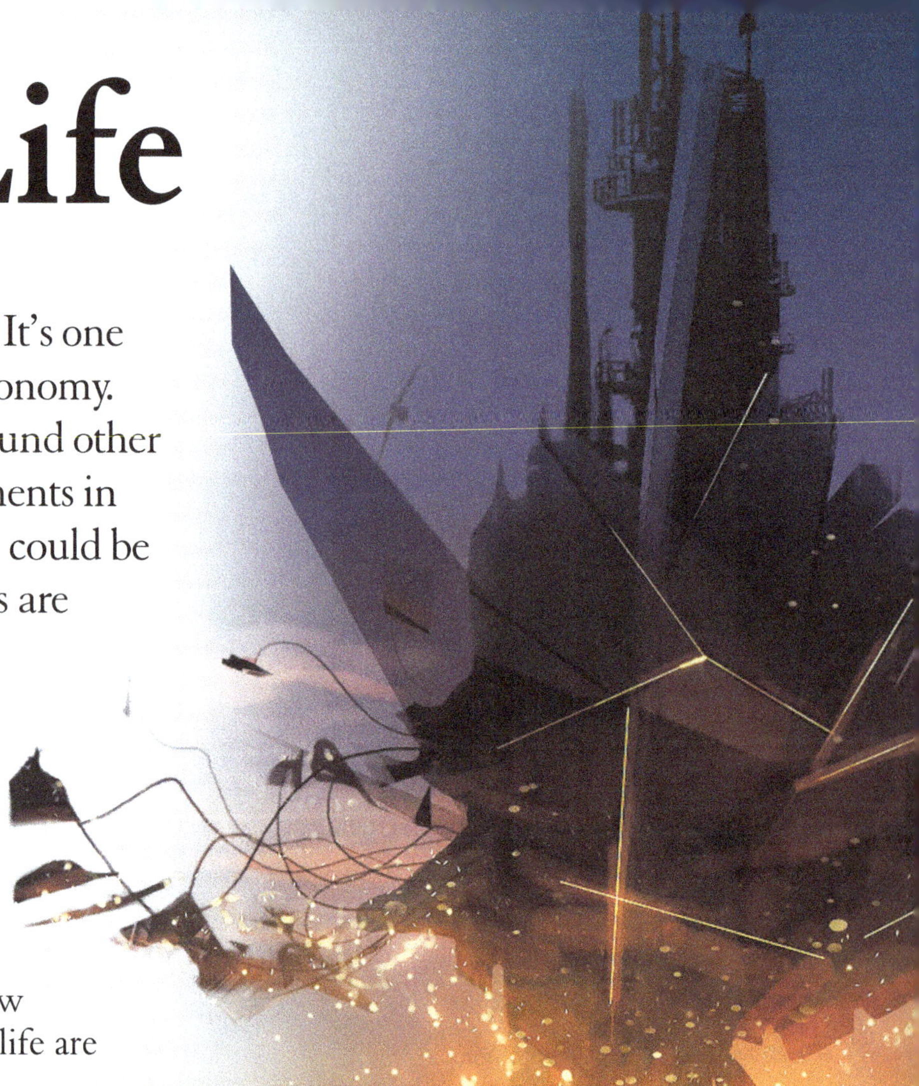

Are we alone in the Universe? It's one of the biggest questions in astronomy. New discoveries of planets around other stars and welcoming environments in our solar system mean that life could be common. But intelligent aliens are a very different matter.

Full of Life?

New discoveries have shown that some bacteria (tiny forms of life) can live in environments that we thought were uninhabitable (impossible to live in). We also now know that the basic chemicals for life are found across our galaxy. If life will automatically happen wherever the conditions are right, then there should be a lot of it in our galaxy.

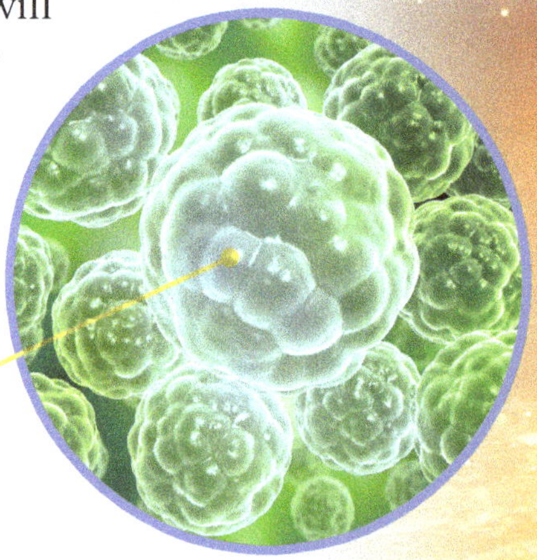

Life would probably start out as simple life forms. However, that doesn't mean that it would develop into the same forms that it has on Earth.

MOON PROFILE

Name: Europa
Moon of: Jupiter
Diameter: 1,900 miles (3,100 km)
Orbital period: 3.55 days
Description: With a deep water ocean and undersea volcanoes beneath its icy crust, there could have been life on Europa

The Gray aliens described by many "alien abduction" victims are more like fairytale monsters than realistic alien life.

Our planet has few resources that any aliens who could travel here would want to take.

Alien invasions are the stuff of movies. Any extraterrestrial species (life forms that aren't from Earth) with the technology to travel between the stars probably wouldn't need to take over other planets.

Alien Invaders

For many years, people have been fascinated by the idea that aliens might want to take over our planet. In reality, an invasion is very unlikely. Travel between star systems is such a huge challenge that it may simply be impossible to do. Hopefully any life forms that were able to reach that level of technology would feel no need to behave in this way toward others.

Did You Know?

There's always more to find out about what lies in the vastness of space. Boost your space knowledge with these amazing facts about our universe.

Our Universe may hold as many as **two trillion** galaxies!

Some astronomers think the Big Bang that started our Universe was just one of many, and that we are a tiny part of an endless "**multiverse**."

Some astronomers think that if the Universe goes on expanding, it could tear itself apart in a **Big Rip**.

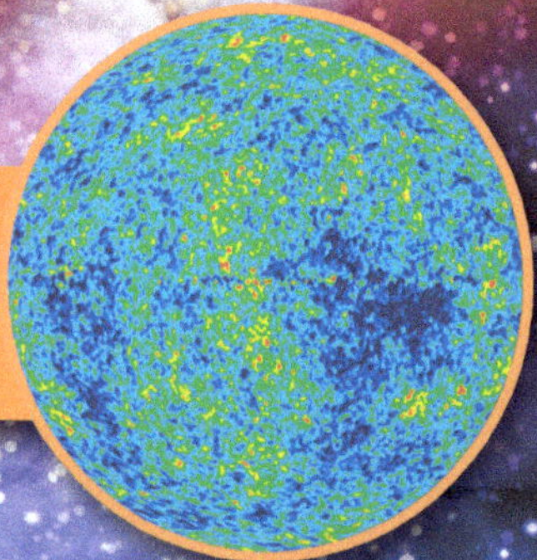

Astronomers believe there are also **dark galaxies**. These are similar to our own Milky Way, but they have hardly any stars, so they are hard to find.

Our own Milky Way galaxy is **crashing** into another (much smaller) galaxy at the moment, and will end up swallowing it completely.

The word "galaxy" comes from the **Greek** for Milky Way.

The Tarantula Nebula's central star cluster is home to the most **massive star** so far discovered—a monster with the mass of about 310 Suns.

Collisions between galaxies often seem to "wake up" their central black holes and turn them into **active galactic cores**.

Astronomers call the undiscovered forms of dark matter **WIMPs**—short for "Weakly Interacting Massive Particles."

At least **six** of the solar system's moons probably have **oceans** hidden beneath their surface.

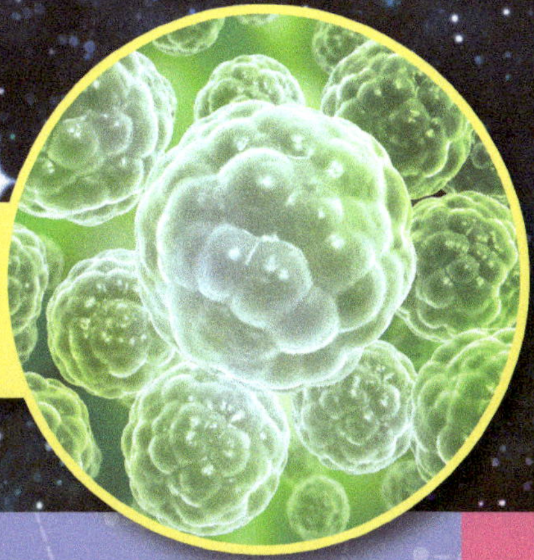

Your Questions Answered

Scientists now know an incredible amount about our universe, but space is still bursting with amazing information. There are always more questions to be answered and this is what makes people want to become scientists and astronauts. Here are the answers to some interesting questions about space, then you can start asking more!

Who named the Milky Way?

The answer is that no one can know for sure. Our galaxy has been called the Milky Way for so long that the origin is lost in history. The Romans called it the "Via Lactea" which means "Road of Milk." The Greeks used the term "Galactos," which means the "milky thing in the sky," and over time this has become our word for all galaxies. The name Milky Way comes from the way the galaxy looks in the night sky—a long, glowing band of stars.

How do I become a space scientist?

The study of space is called astronomy, and space scientists are called astronomers. The most important subjects for an astronomer are the sciences, particularly physics, math, and chemistry. After school, you can go on to study astronomy or physics, or astrophysics—which is a combination of the two!

What are gas and dust clouds made from?

Although space can look empty, it's not. The space we see is actually filled with clouds of dust and gas. The dust is made up of tiny particles of elements such as carbon, iron, magnesium, and silicon. The gas is made up mainly of hydrogen and helium. Scientists spend a long time studying the dust in space, as it contributes to the creation of new planets and stars.

How do new stars form?

Throughout space, there are clouds of dust and gas. Within these clouds, currents and movements can cause dust and gas to group together. They begin to collapse under their own gravity, which causes the core to heat up. Once the newly formed core becomes hot enough, it can resist gravity and stops collapsing, becoming a star.

Is there wind in space? Where does it come from?

The answer is yes, but it's not like the wind we know on Earth. Solar wind is made up of charged particles that move out from the Sun's gravity, and travel across the solar system.

Glossary

asteroid A small rocky object made up of material left over from the birth of the solar system.

atmosphere A shell of gases kept around a planet, star, or other object by its gravity.

black hole A superdense point in space, usually formed by a collapsed core of a giant star. A black hole's gravity is so powerful that even light cannot escape from it.

comet A chunk of rock and ice from the edge of the solar system. Close to the Sun, its melting ices form a coma and a tail.

constellation A star pattern in the sky and the area around it.

dark matter A strange, invisible substance that forms most of the mass in the Universe.

galaxy A large system of stars, gas, and dust with anything from millions to trillions of stars.

gravity A natural force created around objects with mass, which draws other objects toward them.

light-year The distance covered by light in a year—about 5.9 trillion miles (9.5 trillion km).

Milky Way Our home galaxy, a spiral with a bar across its core. Our solar system is about 28,000 light-years from the monster black hole at its heart.

Moon Earth's closest companion in space, a ball of rock that orbits Earth every 27.3 days. Most other planets in the solar system have moons of their own.

nebula A cloud of gas or dust floating in space. Nebulae are the raw material used to make stars.

orbit A fixed path taken by one object in space around another because of the effect of gravity.

planet A world that orbits the Sun, which has enough mass and gravity to pull itself into a balllike shape, and clear space around it of other large objects.

quasar A distant active galaxy with a very bright core.

red dwarf A small, faint star with a cool red surface and less than half the mass of the Sun.

satellite Any object orbiting a planet. Moons are natural satellites made of rock and ice. Artificial (manmade) satellites are machines in orbit around Earth.

spacecraft A vehicle that travels into space.

spiral galaxy A galaxy with a hub of old yellow stars (sometimes crossed by a bar) surrounded by a flattened disk of younger stars, gas, and dust. Bright newborn stars make a spiral pattern across the disk.

supernova An enormous explosion marking the death of a star much more massive than the Sun.

telescope A device that collects light or other radiations from space and uses them to create a bright, clear image. Telescopes can use either a lens or a mirror to collect light.

zodiac Twelve constellations surrounding the Sun's yearly path around Earth's sky. The planets and Moon are usually found within these constellations.

Further Information

BOOKS

Daynes, Katie. *See Inside Space.* London, UK: Usborne Publishing, 2008.

DK Reference. *Space!* New York, NY: DK Publishing, 2015.

Jenkins, Martin. *Exploring Space: From Galileo to the Mars Rover and Beyond.* Somerville, MA: Candlewick Press, 2017.

Murphy, Glenn. *Space: The Whole Whizz-Bang Story* (Science Sorted). New York, NY: Macmillan Children's Books, 2013.

Newman, Ben. *Professor Astro Cat's Frontiers of Space.* London, UK: Flying Eye Books, 2013.

Rogers, Simon. *Information Graphics: Space.* Somerville, MA: Big Picture Press, 2015.

WEBSITES

www.nasa.gov/kidsclub/index.html
Join Nebula at NASA Kids' Club to play games and learn about space.

www.ngkids.co.uk/science-and-nature/ten-facts-about-space
Get started with these ten great facts about space, then explore the rest of the National Geographic Kids site for more fun.

www.esa.int/esaKIDSen/
Explore this site from the European Space Agency. There's information, games, and news.

Index